This Is Not A Rescue

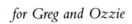

for Greg and Ozzie

This Is Not A Rescue

Emily Blewitt

Seren is the book imprint of
Poetry Wales Press Ltd.
57 Nolton Street, Bridgend, Wales, CF31 3AE
www.serenbooks.com
facebook.com/SerenBooks
twitter@SerenBooks

The right of Emily Blewitt to be identified as
the author of this work has been asserted in accordance
with the Copyright, Designs and Patents Act, 1988.

© Emily Blewitt, 2017

ISBN: 978-1-78172-409-5
ebook: 978-1-78172-413-2
Kindle: 978-1-78172-417-0

A CIP record for this title is available from the British Library.

The publisher acknowledges the financial assistance of the Welsh Books Council.

Cover Image: 'The Bitz' by Karin Jurick

Printed by Airdrie Print Services Ltd.

Contents

This Is Not A Rescue

I want to tell you it will not be as you expect. For years
you have hammered in stakes, handed men the rope and said
consume me with fire. Most have run – one does not burn
a witch lightly. This one is water. He'll unbind you, take
your hands in his and say *remember how you love the ocean?*
Come with me. You'll go to the beach on a cloudy day, watch
foam rise from the sea's churn until sun appears. In turn
you'll say *let's go in* and even though he hesitates, this man
will kick off his shoes and wade to his shins. Jellyfish,
shot with pink like satin dresses, will dance between you, flash
iridescent. His body is all whorls and planes like smoothly sanded
planks used to make a boat, his ears are pale shells you hear
the waves in, he smells of sandalwood and salt, his eyes
are ocean. He'll spot the pebbles that in secret you have sewn
into your skirts and give you his penknife to unpick them.
You can't swim with those. He'll teach you to skim. The pebbles
break the surface like question marks. You'll throw each last one in.

Devouring Jane

Sinewy Willoughby,
thin as a rake, studies my face
like a starving cat.

Darcy abstains,
but owns a library
fat with first editions.

Henry Crawford, hooked on limelight,
scoffs his chips in yesterday's tabloid
and throws up to stay sleek.

Tilney gnaws the bones
of fasting nuns and longs
to carve their virgin hearts.

Wentworth wastes away;
when he drops his pen
through sheer fatigue, my heart leaps

to the pit of my stomach.
Only one satisfies:
Robert Martin,

bare arms like hams,
shirt sleeves rolled up
ready for supper.

Unbuckling his belt
at the prospect of pudding,
he tells me there's no time for poetry

but he'll keep me in steak,
love my brown eyes
that remind him of cows.

Woman Poet

They say she *smouldered*, her long blonde hair
shook over one shoulder, her blue-black jeans
a second skin. She read a poem

sounding out her name, flung it
boomerang through the auditorium
and those heels, by God those heels

were a stiletto pressed to the artery,
made pulses quick-quick slow
with each step forward. She'd not look back.

She unzipped her lipsticked smile mid-air, slow-motion;
I felt it pass my lips on its somersault out.
It landed, caught, bowed its ovation.

She threw her head back, opened her throat
like a kookaburra in a tree full of snakes
and laughed. *Smouldering?*

She was a wild bitch howling, the bush on fire,
her lyrics mouthed into wind-song,
her sentence ending on a question.

Wrecker

For you, I'll light beacons.
Wait for my signal –

I'll beckon you in.
Will you come to me

smiling, lightly recall
that we've been here before;

walked, hand in hand,
clutching our shoes?

Come. Here,
I'll take you

freighted with silk,
eyes round like coins.

I'll strike from your finger
the ring that she gave you;

watch while you flounder,
waves rise to claim you.

Boy, when you drown
no soul shall save you.

I Threw Myself at You

Like a knife at a turning wheel
Like a die on green felt
Like a kiss across a crowded room
Like an axe into a great oak door
Like a stick of chalk at a child's head
Like a voice inside a doll, inside a chest
Like the shadow on a bedsheet hung outside
Like an apple with a worm inside
Like spit from a skyscraper
Like an egg at a window
Like a poltergeist
Like a baited hook
Like a javelin
Like yellow roses
Like confetti
Like the baby and the bathwater
Like the man from the ledge
Like that Other Woman
Like me

How to Marry a Welsh Girl

It's not so much about asking permission
as thieving. For dowry you take what you can,
get what you're given: the chapel, prolific sheep, jackdaws, circling
hills and black mountains, the usual ropey singing
at the pub they don't speak English in, cheese and pickle
cocktail sticks, pasties, corned beef. I book the catering
because the handsome pizza boys my mam eyes up for my sister ask,
Do you know the Evanses from Porthyrhyd? My second cousin Daniel?
At Llanarthne the village hall welcomes us with palms open –
their best tea set and crockery will cost us a song.

Cariad, it's not so much about Welshing
as fleecing. My heart lies cooling on the griddle
next to the currant-filled cakes. Here's a hint: I'm stirring
the cawl or knitting socks in a corner, disguised as an old woman
in a tall black hat. If you still want me, you'll have to make off with me,
and even then my da and brawd won't give up the chase. If I tear my dress
while getting away, that's love; if I keep myrtle in my bouquet,
we'll grow sons. Since you're a *Saes* you won't know
to carve a lovespoon, but I'll tell you that birdsong in the morning
means luck; there might be donations of cheese, money, wool, bacon.

The Walking Wed

So it's arrived: the zombie apocalypse. The trick
is to keep moving: like guests at a wedding,
we begin at the bar and creep past
sweating ushers who know their turn is coming –
inexorably coming, staggering and shunting
towards them like an old train carriage or a barge
on a canal through a tunnel. That's us:
on our backs, slowly, achingly, walking through darkness
until the world is light again, the birds announce
our presence and the sun makes red its promise
to sting us. We'll keep fit and fast and endure
like marathon runners: our bones will sharpen;
our flesh fall away. We'll look for the fight
in us, in others like us. We'll carry weapons
or things that can be used as weapons. We'll take
up baseball, boxing; come out swinging. We'll live
off flumps and tins of beans abandoned in corner shops
and supermarkets. We'll celebrate our victory
in football stadiums, make hearts with hands
for an imagined sea of faces. #BetterTogether.
We'll score. We'll dance. We'll flourish
like weeds, our roots deep as brainstems. We'll build a boat
that's not quite big enough. Me, you, the cat. At the end
they'll tie cans to us. We'll rattle. We'll run.

Navigation Points

Crossing the bridge, you find me
by touch alone; have turned off
your sat nav, dipped your lights.
You feel your way
past landmarks, signs,
the steady flow
of traffic.

When you arrive, though,
I am still at the threshold.
Standing by streetlight,
I think I am lost.

You smile, then,
lead me gently inside;
draw the curtains,
undress me by sight.

You lower your long dark lashes
just once: to trace your route
across my skin.
These moles, you say,
fine points for navigation.

You'll *map my constellations*, you explain,
know me anywhere.

Salt Roses

I lowered you gentle
so the water lapped your hurt,

dipped a pockmarked plastic jug
to the brim, and tried to draw

the pain, the skin
at the small of your back,

where the bloom was:
where your roots dug deep

while thorns beneath
pressed on, up, towards the sun

which smeared the bathroom wall
in thick gold streaks

and made salt roses
of your cheeks.

I saw then how it must have been:
soft woollen mitts at night, cool calamine;

that small sequestered scar
at your jaw, dancing the lip-line.

Florence

For F.G.D.

Your mother will tell you
you slept through it all,
coiled as a curl
tucked neatly behind
her delicate ear;

that you did not hear
the vows that were spoken,
or witness the joining of hands,
her elegant dress, the statement she made
in her shocking-pink coat;

that, while you lay
pressed as a flower she kept
from her wedding bouquet –
with your first picture,
a crisp silhouette –

she stood at the threshold, waving,
waving, waiting for you to arrive.

Still Life

In the cradle
they gave you, your head
rested round as a peach, so
perfect, they said, we could eat you.
You were delicate, sweet; slept still
as a seed. Through glass, we watched
you ripen to a bright banana-yellow;
your blackberry eyes open
to smile, then crease in a cry.
There were strawberry prints
where forceps had
freed you.

The Philobrutist

Give me the man who keeps a lead in the boot of his car for rescuing
loose dogs. I want him crouching, shooing daft pairs of ducks
out of oncoming traffic; I want the pavement lined with dandelions
he steps deftly over, open-palmed.

I want his humane mousetraps, the miniature fences he makes
from Cadbury's fingers, to send him out jogging at 3am,
so two fat rodents can taste chocolate and freedom
in a wildflower meadow. I want him to fix a broken radio

and rig up three extension cables from the garage, so a budgerigar
can sing and bob and see out of a window.
I want his unerring, unnerving birdsong whistle;
I want him to bathe his mum's tortoise every morning

and dry her carefully on old newspaper, while explaining
how her shell's nerve-endings respond unexpectedly to touch.
I want him when he matter-of-factly puts peanut butter sandwiches
out for the badgers. I want him to lay his hands

on my shoulders and loosen the knot at the nape of my neck and I want
to stand on his feet while he spins me in circles. I want him so badly
I'm giddy and ravenous; I want him to follow me,
follow me home.

Lines

about one of your features, perhaps
your eyes.

                    Your eyes are blue as a match-day sky.
Or your hands;

                they're pianist's.

My love, I'll warn you:
poets are sly;
this gift would unwrap you
with a piece missing.

                You have a beard,
                two tattoos, a cat called Brian.
                You like shirts checked
                like picnic blankets.

I'll open you there, trace

                your tattoos,
            cup your bearded jaw
in my palms while Brian looks on
                and your fingers perform
                slow arpeggios
                on the arch of his back.

What can I say? I'm lost, I love
your missing piece, the part I love like
                the part I love
                  where your hair recedes
as it shows me more of you,
          is showing me more of you,
                more than this poem,
                more than I know.

Witness

For C.B.

Word spread quickly
that winter:
your car, abandoned,
the driver's side
a gaping mouth
to your graceful vault
over the barrier,
towards the river.
I knew, then,
you would transform;
could, if I wanted,
watch you change

from the tall
coat-hanger boy
perched on the edge
of his desk, beautiful
bones planed sharp
through his sweater,
hands slim and sure,
gently holding
a clarinet (its reed
pressed to his lips,
in-breath)

to a cormorant,
made fearless, still
as though carved
on that bank, dripping.
I could see
your slick head
glancing the surface,
barely a ripple.
Wings tucked
for the dive.

Burry Port

After Andrew Greig

It is the lighthouse, the harbour walls
kids jump in summer, the old boats in a line,
broken rudders and faded buoys.

It is *Cefn Sidan* leading to the dunes, beacons lit by wreckers,
terraced houses squinting, blinkered, blocked drains
and seagull squalls.

It is the homewreckers, the women who swap and squabble
amongst themselves, stage-whisper about their neighbours,
who *just can't leave it*
                    alone, like the old stray

who wanders through the village, collecting scraps
and kicks, his eyes sad, his coat brindled, the salt and vinegar
of yesterday's chips, the sand and headland.

How to Explain *Hiraeth* to an Englishman

Take greyhounds. Ignore the words your village vicar slurred about souls from his tired pulpit all those years ago in Wrington; instead consider that greyhounds make excellent pets. They can be friends with other greyhounds, children and cats. Though they can reach speeds of up to 40mph, greyhounds are couch potatoes. Greyhounds are stylish, frequently seen wearing scarves, snoods and leg warmers. Greyhounds are sight hounds and can sometimes lose their way.

To find a greyhound, you can follow the smell of chips into Cardiff town centre, or google Greyhound Rescue Centre Wales. Names for greyhounds include Ballymac Kay, Coppice Socks, Stanley, Pat, Witches Bravo, Tipex and Noodles. My favourite greyhound is Noodles – the advert says you can just add hot water and chaos ensues and shows him nose to nose with three pampered cats on a bed. Apparently he needs a bit of training to become 'a more balanced diet'.

Once, I was leant on by a greyhound dozing standing up, and when he opened his eyes I swear they said *hiraeth*.

So when you puzzle through these streets, feeling lost to this west country that is no West Country, look into the eyes of that animal, the one whose coat is mottled fawn, brindle-flanked so you can count each rib, whose longing burns in muscled limbs and who quietly sits, politely waiting, knowing beneath his homeless layers that greyhounds cannot live outdoors, that greyhounds make excellent pets.

Moses

Dad, when we said we'd found him in a cardboard box,
down soggy streets in pouring rain, what we meant was
he needed a home.

Mum knew you'd say *no, no more*, unless
there was no choice, unless it was you or the road –
and so, since no one wants a weekend father

we said we'd found him curled up small, a ball
of wispy, near-blown fluff: abandoned, lost,
with wide sad eyes he opened to please you.

Of course it worked. As soon as you named him
this wily cocksure little cat unfurled, expanded
to fill the space left in your lap,

where, stretched supine, sunny-side up,
he purred his gratitude, washed his paws just enough
and earned his stripes with easy grace.

Not Lost

Mum tells me she'll walk into the woods.
When the time comes, she'll unhook her mac,
leave the door on the latch and not come back

just like old Tom, who disappeared one day
and the next we found him stretched out in the sun
of next door's greenhouse, fur still warm and fading

from glossy black to Saharan dirt.
I tell Mum of where the big cats stalk, eyes full
of fire for bison, buffalo, the antelope leaping skywards…

how the Maasai lay their dead out in the open bush
with a single pair of sandals and a stick, to ascend to the heavens,
become great herders of the burning stars.

The Search

The village is out.
There are stars, houses
wrapped in snow. A search begins.
Faces moon at windows, burgled torchlight skirts
the ceilings, and here, I light candles
from stubs. Mute as ink, we peer
into this winter-dark, wait
for flashing yellow,
men, their lights.

Sometimes I Think of Chapel

And the vestry's cold echo, the slap-slapping
of sandals on flagstones, the Sunday School
Bell. Me in frock and frilly socks, holding
my cool green leather *Caniedydd yr Ifanc* as I wonder
about what comes afterwards, the chocolate egg I'll crack
on the kitchen counter, my fingerprints smudging its sheen,
my mouth forming the Welsh nestled in my throat
and then flying out to the ceiling,

> a bright new bird.

And I think of my mother, leading me by the hand
up the aisle for the last time, after it had all come out,
what her Uncle did to her, the congregation watching,
and how she looks back at the pulpit and prays
She'll never need them,

> *let her never learn to kneel.*

Forgiveness

I am my mother's daughter. I forgive
the man, my grandmother who let him in,
who called my mother *a bloody liar*
years later, when she told

of the waking nights, cold and gagged
by her nightgown's shroud.
How could your mother sleep? the man argued,
reasonably, holding his denial

as though carefully turning
a bedroom door handle, his knuckles white.
And though I was too small to know why,
I understood that absent grandmothers

were silent, and some nights in dreams
I'd wake whispering her name.
I grew, bereaved and strong as a sapling
away from that house, in my mother's love.

But I am my father's daughter, too. I won't
forget. Every night,
I bury the man alive and breathing.
My fires burn hotter than any crematorium.

Homecoming

You are man, now.
Stand upright as this house
you were born in, your arms
these green oak beams
which hold us, as you take me

through the finish:
the fine brushed grain
of my smooth round belly,
a perfect curve
so rare in carpentry.

Yet I am undone, too –
frayed as this half-finished shawl
I am knitting, my hands
scrabbling for spools,
unravelling thread –

how you were carried
the Welsh way,
slung high on the hip.
Your cheek to my breast,
crumpled as cloth.

When in Recovery

Get out of bed. Feed the cat.
Add a level teaspoon of sugar to builder's tea and stir clockwise.
Resist the urge to stick your knife in the toaster.
Be reckless enough to descend hills at a decent pace
but pick your mountains wisely. Get out of breath.
Focus on words, wasting them. Take citalopram –
four syllables, once a day, behind the tongue.
Understand that there are days you watch yourself
as though you are a balloon held aloft your body
by a slip of string you fear will break.
Grow your hair. Buy exotic oils at discount stores
and comb them through. Think in colour. Sit in the salon and explain
no blue is blue enough now. Try red – pillar-box, satanic red.
Enjoy the sharp press of the needle, its single tear of blood
when you pierce your nostril. Put a diamond in it so it winks.
Accept that sun-worship is good, the Vitamin D produces serotonin
and sensation. When you cry, howl at the moon.
Wear your rituals lightly. At the end of each day, step out of them
as though they're expensive silk lingerie.

Giving

I give you, this:
cold, hard earth;
the bear beneath

who would shrink to the shape of a sack
to let one cub breathe
in winter,

and, come thaw, emerge
all eyes and teeth,
head for water.

There: watch her
snatch from the air
a fish, mid-leap.

See how carefully
she keeps her ears dry.

The Question

So she's twenty-one,
bored and lonely,
working in an office

beside a man
who takes his coffee
with vanilla syrup, and flashes

a lopsided smile
through broken sips
every time she glances up.

He's a man who wants
her opinion on how best
to phrase a sentence

asking someone important
for something trivial,
and who puts his hand

on her shoulder,
her wrist;
that's how it begins.

He's a man
who shares himself
like he rolls cigarettes

and though she can't ignore
the paunch,
his poor work ethic,

the steady girlfriend
he's just moved in with,
she doesn't complain

about it, no, or when
this man's roaming
Blackberry interrupts

her thought
while the office hums
and his large, constant,

clumsy hands paw at
the glass of his tablet,
drum the keyboard,

thump the desk
and finger his phone.
It goes on

and she's flattered, right,
this twenty-one-year-old
bored and lonely woman

in a junior office position
who's just trying to fund
an expensive education?

An Away Day comes.
She assumes

he's all mouth
and no trousers.
She's only half right.

The knock
is almost inaudible
and yet she answers,

through curiosity
more than anything:
crosses her arms

over her nightdress
while he stands there,
hands open – reaching

clumsily for her,
eyes pools of slurry,
pout a hard wet red.

He steps inside
and sprawls
on her half-made bed.

And it's just at this moment
she asks herself,
Do I consent?

When I Think of Bald Men

I think of vultures, the misunderstood deep-cleaners
of the Sahara, immune to disease. The ones who orderly gather
in committees, who are proud of their collective nouns:
a *venue, kettle*, or *volt* of vultures putting together

the agenda before arranging sandwiches for delegates
and mince pies at Christmas; vultures photocopying *Any Other Business*
in Confidential purple; vultures washing-up and picking-clean
leftovers in the staffroom, at the buffet table; a wake of vultures

that dance, dad-style in lines, or bob their heads to a kill in time
to the music. Vultures that shout *And all's weeeellll!* at 3am
after the Office Christmas Party; vultures that tidy up the mess
in the Ladies made by a gaggle of geese, parliament of owls, an exultation

of larks, brood of chickens, tiding of magpies, a murder of crows...
Vultures with their trousers rolled up, showing milk-bottle legs;
vultures with laughter-lines and wrinkled backs-of-necks;
vultures that are nicknamed *Bearded Vulture,*

Slender-Billed Vulture, Red-Headed Vulture, White-Rumped Vulture
by their vulture friends. Every office has some –
you know the men I mean. The ones that are reluctant
to fly; the ones that hiss when threatened.

Brief Encounter

He's being unfaithful.
I find lipstick smears at the corners of his whiskers,
a silk nightgown pooled at the bottom of our wardrobe
as though flung there after an assignation.

One afternoon, I come home to the laundry pile
turned-upside, skirts and stockings scattered, trousers stepped-out-of,
my favourite blouse unbuttoned and crumpled
and the ironing board still in its cupboard.

There are traces everywhere: between bedclothes, sheets,
the inside of socks and the gussets of knickers.
I fume, *Why is everything I own covered in your hair?*
And someone's moved my red velvet sling-backs!

Eventually, the other shoe drops.
He wants to be caught. So let's get this over with;
I conveniently forget my best leather handbag, swing by
and find him sashaying up and down

a catwalk, wearing one of my dresses.
I get no apology. He wants me to say
There's been no adultery; of course you can borrow my things.
I say, *You can walk in heels?!*

He grins, flashes my own patent knee-highs
that reach to his groin; kicks a pointed toe
to his ear and washes his arse.
All cats are kings and this one's in drag.

The Couple Opposite

leave their curtains open and the lights on.
Their front room is a home cinema.
They play videos of themselves on an overhead projector
and sit up airbrushing their flaws.
They have removed cellulite, body hair, wrinkles and excess skin.
They use empty picture frames and incredulous hats as props
and have taped black crosses on the carpet.
They chew the scenery so much they leave bite marks in it.
They are their very own script supervisors, though have trouble
differentiating between the safe and live area.
Their special effects are basic, and they like squibs.
They don't have children, though last week
they affected stardom and adopted a cat, put a lead on it
and sat on the doorstep, waiting for the paparazzi.
The cat made a run for it, but was eventually retrieved.

Boba Fett and the Sarlacc

He's the man you wait for,
who's in your sights.
A man who reads the world
from behind his visor, who looks out

for number one. He's smart –
he'll track a falcon
across galaxies, set an ambush,
close a trap.

He knows what a uniform's for,
and it's not for keeping white.
He cradles his blaster, cocks his head
to one side, then the other.

Man of few words.
He's no good to me dead.
He's a badass but no scoundrel,
plays the odds but doesn't brag.

And when he falls into you, plunges
to your death's head,
you taste his manhood.
You suck and suck and suck.

Lamnidae

When you dive you look for the largest female:
the most confident ambush predator.
You clip mirrors on your camera, watch
for shadows, an inexplicable chill in temperature.
Your interpretation is practised, based on experience:
the unlucky, the ones who failed

my body, the way it turns swiftly
at the last moment, as if in tango;
my seductive fins lowered, their black tips pointing
to the ocean bed, my spine made rigid
from desire, mouth open as though about to
speak it. I can feel the thrum of your heart

beneath your cage of ribs, the electrical storm
behind your glass eyes trying to make sense of it.
Mammal, you are clumsy in your skin
as the runt of the litter that cape seals kill.
Pup, see these teeth in half-smile,
touch this sandpaper skin.

My eyes roll back.
What makes you think you are safe?
What if I told you the world's an ocean?

On Watching *Paranormal Witness*

It begins conventionally, with an unexpected turn
of events: a young family new to town, forced to look
for a home. The house they find is empty, cheap

as chips and chipped all over: old panels, damp; nothing that a lick
of paint and some love won't fix, they think. If it were me
I'd wonder what the catch was. As it is, Americans –

they're optimists. The glass – half-full – shatters
and milk-white plates fling themselves at the wall. Before long,
the kitchen smells of death. Lamps blink SOS, the TV switches itself off

and on again, off and on again. The attic door slams from its hinges;
the grandfather clock stops at 3.07. Birds strike at the windows.
If there's a family dog – God help. The local priest

bears witness, yes; a psychic meets them half-way. *Did you know
your house was built on sacred burial land?* Cue talking heads.
The dénouement waits. The kids are scared of what their parents think

are ghosts. I can't help but think of worse: what if
the shadow stranger creeping into your son's bedroom is no demon,
but a favourite uncle; what if the smell of meat is on his hands?

Things My Dance Teacher Used to Say

Chassés are chasing steps

To spiral, you spin slowly and trail your pointed foot

Practise standing on one leg

Use contrary body motion

Your arms should show control and musical interpretation

If you don't like me smoking, sit over there

It shouldn't burn

Keep your eyes up

You're blushing again

You're as flat-chested as I am

If you don't use it you lose it

If you don't click this time, there's something wrong with you

You're too naïve

You're not afraid to swing those hips

I was a loose cannon

I used to sprint barefoot at school

You remind me of me when I was your age

If I had my time again, I'd be a historian

Use resistance

It takes a bit of grit to make a pearl

Self-Defence

The instructor tells us
Imagine you're on the telephone, holding
an ice cream with the other hand.
Get into your fighting stance.
You have four scoops
(strawberry, chocolate, rum and raisin,
mint choc chip) so don't drop
your guard. We're not pretending we're ninjas here
but you have to breathe like one,
push the air between your teeth and clench
those glutes. Now jab –
cross – jab – cross – aim for the solar plexus,
ribs, chest. Uppercut to the chin, if you do it right
their teeth could sever their tongue,
give them a left hook, slam their temple in.
Knock 'em dead. Block with your elbow,
bob and duck when you have to.
Now flick your knee like the lash of a whip
cracked against a sailor's chest, curl your toes back,
kick like an axe. Execute, again. Cut their legs out
under them with your foot-sword.
Your partner's going to come at you and you're going to
send them flying into next week.
When you roundhouse, you're spinning 360 degrees
smashing all the cups in your kitchen.
Walk forward on your hands to the top of a press-up
and pick up the pieces. You are a bridge,
a plank you must cross to meet
your kick-ass self. If you wanted nice,
you'd have gone for tea and cake instead.
Remember Buffy? Forget the ice cream, imagine
you have a sharpened stake and a crucifix.
Aim straight for that virgin heart.

Resolution

I will make myself Morticia Addams.
I will grow my hair to my waist, wear

floor-length black velvet.
I will smoke.

I will hang gilded mirrors, watch myself
pass without reflection.

I will slowly descend great staircases, intricately laced
with antique cobwebs.

I will hold brief but meaningful conversations
with the spiders.

My house will be ruined;
my underwear immaculate.

The bed in which I wrap my tongue
around my husband's French

will be cast iron, four-postered,
shrouded in silk.

We Broke Up

Because my cat
screamed her passion on our lawn

Because bears
don't wet their ears

Because great white sharks
swim solitary lives

Because blue whales' tongues
lie heavy

Because barnacles
have no true heart

Because elephants
mourn their dead

Because dogs
love unconditionally

Because tortoises
feel their shells being touched

Because rabbits
breed like rabbits

Because fox sex
hurts

Because ducks
are rapists

Because cows
hold grudges

Because roe deer
lower heads in prayer

Because wild boar
are matriarchal

Because domestic rats
live and die in pairs

Because giant pandas
don't conceive on camera

Because emperor penguins
clutch eggs between their feet

Because honey bees
die when they love

Because crows
mate for life

Because my heart
made the sound an animal makes

Because of crows, the shadows
of crows

Dear Emily

You have that look again. You're all steamed-up.
The medicine cabinet is a curiosity, encasing reflections
you don't recognise. It is as though someone has smudged you
with greasy fingers. You wash compulsively, repeat
each barbed stroke twice, for luck. You are afraid
of being collared, of getting stuck inside these walls,
the painted ceiling instead of stars, this home and its cat flap
locked. You search for a window, a high ledge to climb
and watch woodlice, which drive you wild
with their gliding across the carpet as though on coasters,
muscles rippling like racehorses. They tumble
from the curtains, belly-up, legs pedalling the air
before curling to a pill and bouncing, charcoal shells intact.
They prove hard to kill. You spend days trying
and sometimes cry at nights. One leap
and you could breach the sill, your voice a fracture,
louder, rising. Will you fall the way that cats do,
arch your spine in a defiant, graceful twist
and land on your feet?

Gifts from Crows

i.

My friend the crow has many names.
When I find him, he's lost some feathers,
gained a limp. He squawks his dismay
but lets me lift him; he perches
on my shoulder, brushes my cheek
as if kissing.

I feed him titbits until he fattens.
It becomes harder to hold up
my head when he speaks.
I'm thin as bone, eat like him.
He cracks words like nuts
with his flintlock beak.

At the doctor's he swallows
my secrets and preens
his immaculate blue-black coat.
Later, he says, *You're not pregnant*.
I know, I say, but we take the test anyway.

When he broods in the crawlspace beneath my ribs
his wings beat my heart's tattoo. If he stops,
I'll leave, I think.

One day he takes off, and returns with gifts:
spreads his wings in courtly supplication, bows low
and winks. He locates what's lost, what's missing: a key,
the odd earring, a bottle cap bright as an engagement ring.
He puts seeds in my mouth, caws
Eat, eat.

ii.

The crow's mate arrives, calling
his name, over and over.

She sits on my shoulder and nibbles
my ear. She's bigger than him; heavier.
Her gifts are practical: the polished skull of a vole,
a piece of string, an empty packet of aspirin.
She mimics foxes, traffic;
when I step out from the pavement she screams
Brake! Brake!

We go back to the doctor's.

In the waiting room
she flicks through the women's magazines
and solves puzzles;

you can tell she's thinking
as she clacks her tongue against her beak.

When I collect my prescriptions I see

her: she blinks in and out of focus, haunts
the edges, the tail of my eye.

Later, we hunker down at the base
of my spine, brace for the blow.

The numbness waits
like a worm for rainfall.

iii.

The crows are nesting. I worry
about them, their fledgling young.

Like all new parents, they wing it.

He seems proud, has puffed out
his chest; he scouts for worms,

loops circles through the trees

like a trapeze artist.
She gives her gifts
                by sleight-of-beak.

On the ground,
I am the colour of eggshells;
my hair sticks up like their chick's.

I work and work to pierce the membrane.

They recognise my face,
                have learned to speak
        my name.

iv.

One on each shoulder, at dawn and dusk,
my familiar shadows bring me tidings.

This week, a woman in a brown coat
put a gull out of its misery,

gathered its broken umbrella body
in her arms like a sleeping child

and walked home slowly.
They watched her bury him.

They chatter of pigeons squabbling,
how the seagull's delicate rain-dance

brings up ground-held grubs,
the magpies bob like barristers,

the excitable table-manners of starlings,
the mating habits of ducks.

And a buzzard was sighted
not far from here, circling.

A raven was caged
until her feathers grew back.

Honeyguide

I am the honeyguide who waits on the wind
for your shrill catcall clamour.

I am the honeyguide, whose unremarkable brown feathers draw you
to gather, taste some of the wildness this land has to offer.

I am the one who warns you of desiring too much, who picks out
the grubs from hexagon chambers and chatters of crumbs.

I have danced this path for thousands of years, I'll tell you
your future, I know by heart that promises matter.

I am the honeyguide you whistle to, cast out your invisible net for,
wind the thread that leads to the humming of bees

whose barbs would kill me, whose sweetness lies buried, sticky
as honey.

My Colours

Love, I'll show you

first, on my right forearm
a peacock in jade and gold
so when I flick my wrist its feathers

                                        fan   out
like the winning hand at cards

on my left breast
in oyster-grey
beats the anatomical diagram
of a heart

on my right breast
Blodeuwedd
the owl girl with amber eyes
becomes roses
                lavender
                foxgloves
                daisies

on my collarbone
a cicada sings

across my back
a tiger stalks
                to hide
                        the scars

while in plain sight
between my shoulder blades
two white wings
                    take   off

coiled around my inner thigh
a snake hisses
                bottle-green

at my hips
           macaws kiss

above my womb
the moon waits
in all
          her   phases

on my right foot
a greyhound sprints
           straight off   the blocks

at my left heel
curls a brown hare
               and an orange fox

Love, when I show you
           my colours

I am an ephemera
of red kites
        wheeling
              through stormy skies

I am a riot
       a cacophony
           a bird of paradise

a gilded kingfisher
        diving blue

One in Three Billion

i.

I am a woman
of childbearing age.

You pitch your purr
into darkness

at the same frequency
a newborn child cries

for its mother.
Was it longing

for a baby
that made me drive,

single-handedly,
from the rescue centre,

my fingers through the bars
of your carrier,

all the way home?

ii.

Your adoptive father considers
banning you from our bedroom
but it's no good –
you won't be shut out,
you squeeze in
through the tiniest gaps,
push your snout past tangled limbs
to the space between coccyx and pelvis,
heavy-footed, unsubtle, oh how you
always manage to stand exactly
on the centre of my nipple.

iii.

I think I must
be one in three billion

infected with that parasite,
toxoplasma gondii,

particularly interesting to study
in women of childbearing age.

Apparently it can lead
to reckless behaviour,

potentially even anxiety
disorders, depression,

schizophrenia.
It also provokes

a form of neuroticism
called 'guilt-proneness',

which might explain
how I feel

when I carefully shake
you out of my lap

to relieve
a full bladder.

iv.

You smell of cat:
a baked-loaf animal,
of warm spittle
on your tongue

and flanks.
Today, I linger
near the scabs
at your collar

and part your coat
against the grain.
This would usually
have you sweeping

off – offended – but
today you don't budge:
you're dog-tired,
eyes practically rolling

back in your head
and I catch a single,
small flea, crack it
between fingernails.

We have an understanding,
you and I:
you put up with
the poems
and I
crack the fleas.

Notes

'Wrecker' nods to Pembrey's beach, *Cefn Sidan*, which is reputed to have provided some villagers with careers as wreckers. In the early nineteenth century, the '*Gwyr-y-Bwelli Bach*' ('People with Little Hatchets') lit beacons in order to attract ships, before raiding them when they foundered.

Some of the nuptial traditions described in 'How to Marry a Welsh Girl' are real.

'Burry Port' was inspired by Andrew Greig's poem 'Orkney/This Life'.

'*Hiraeth*' is one of those untranslatable Welsh words; it roughly means 'the soul's longing for home'.

Caniedydd yr Ifanc is a book of hymns for young singers.

Boba Fett and the Sarlacc feature in the original *Star Wars* trilogy. Boba Fett is a helmeted bounty hunter, while the Sarlacc is a large tentacled creature that resembles a carnivorous plant and is buried beneath the desert sand. In *Episode VI: Return of the Jedi*, Boba Fett falls into the Sarlacc's open mouth.

Lamnidae are a family of shark, to which great white sharks belong.

Paranormal Witness is an American documentary series for television, featuring eyewitness accounts and reconstructions of paranormal activity.

Toxoplasma gondii is a tiny parasite that infects the cells of up to 50% of the world's population, and is especially associated with cats. It reputedly can affect the behaviour of its hosts in order to reproduce – making mice, for instance, become more reckless and more likely to be eaten.

Acknowledgements

Acknowledgements are due to the editors of the following publications, in which some of these poems (or versions of them) first appeared: *The Forward Book of Poetry 2017, The Interpreter's House, Cheval, Poetry Wales, The Rialto, Prole, Ambit, Furies, Nu2: Memorable Firsts, Brittle Star, Sentinel Literary Quarterly, The Woven Tale Press, And Other Poems, Hinterland, Cadaverine, Pomegranate*. Roy Marshall, Kim Moore and Carolyn Jess-Cooke all published some of these poems on their websites. 'Woman Poet' was first written as part of a collaboration with Rebecca Parfitt entitled 'The Changing Habits of Women' for the Enemies/*Gelynion* project.

'This Is Not A Rescue' was Highly Commended in the 2016 Forward Prizes, having being nominated by Josephine Corcoran at *And Other Poems*. 'Still Life' won the *Cadaverine*/Unity Day Poetry Competition in 2010. 'The Walking Wed' was shortlisted in the 2017 York Literature Festival/YorkMix Poetry Competition. 'Resolution' was Highly Commended in the 2014 Terry Hetherington Award; 'How to Explain *Hiraeth* to an Englishman' and 'The Philobrutist' were both Commended in the 2015 Terry Hetherington Award.

This collection would not have been possible without the love and support of those closest to me, especially my parents, siblings and in-laws. You know who you are and in which poems you appear (forgive me). Feline family members have also provided inspiration and warmth on cold evenings, especially Moz (who was Found in a Box). Thank you to all of my friends who have been interested in and excited about the book.

I would like to thank also the readers and mentors who offered advice: Kim Moore, who pushed me to submit and perform and improve; members of the poetry group at Grange-over-Sands and at Aldeburgh; InkSplott (Christina Thatcher, Susie Wild, Mark Blayney, Kate North, Hilary Watson, clare e. potter, Katherine Stansfield, Rebecca Parfitt); those poets who participated in the 2016 Seamus Heaney Poetry Summer School at Queen's University, Belfast. Roy Marshall gets a special shout-out for reading through and annotating the whole damn manuscript with impressive clarity and sensitivity. Katherine Stansfield and Davd Towsey helped me find the perfect cover image. Aida Birch, Carolyn Jess-Cooke and Jonathan Edwards provided encouragement and references. Amy Wack, extraordinary editor and fellow cat-lover, was marvellous.

Last but not least, this book is dedicated to my husband, Greg Young, and our rescue feline, Ozzie. Both have provided all sorts of inspiration and love, too numerous to list. Both rescued me.